OEMCO

SOMETHING'S WRONG IN MY HOUSE

By Katherine Leiner

Photographs By Chuck Gardner

FRANKLIN WATTS
NEW YORK/LONDON/TORONTO/SYDNEY
1988

Cover design by Paul Tanck

Library of Congress Cataloging-in-Publication Data
Leiner, Katherine.
    Something's wrong in my house / Katherine Leiner.
        p.   cm.
    Bibliography: p.
    Summary: Eight young people describe life in a family in which
alchoholism is a problem; the effects on the other family members,
and the help they have found in coping with the situation.
    ISBN 0-531-10506-7
    1. Children of alcoholics—United States—Juvenile literature.
2. Children of alcoholics—Services for—United States—Directories.
[1. Alcoholics.   2. Alcoholism.   3. Children's writings.]
I. Title.   87-25163
HV5132.L44 1988   CIP
362.2′92—dc19   AC

This book is dedicated to my sister,
Marie, with love. Together, we were
both the witnesses and the victims.
At least now we know we are not alone.

Author's Note

To protect the anonymity so important in recovery, the children pictured throughout this book are models and serve only to represent the actual children of alcoholics.

Katherine Leiner

CONTENTS

ACKNOWLEDGMENTS

Of the many to whom I am indebted, I want to give special thanks to the following, who gave so generously of their time, expertise and skills.

Brentwood Art School, Eric Chinski, Jill Deleau, Kelli Doty, Rebecca Fox, Gina Gardner, Julien Gervreau, Marie Gewirtz, Linda Goldman, Mary Lee Gowland, the Greifs, Cynthia, Guy, and Ceci Greenbaum, William Inglis, Gretta Keene, Majory Kline, Dylan Leiner, Barbara Lembeck, Peter Levitt, Jerry Moe and *Kids are Special*, Beverly Moore and the Girls Club, Liza Murrow, Miriam Rodriguez, Galen Shostac, Dr. Richard Shuman, Joey Sorrentino, Bonnie Thompson's Tuesday night ACA group, the Trachtenbergs, Rene, Matthew, and Sarah Wager, Lynn Webster, Sarah Willens, Shirley Windward, Dr. Helen Wolff, Ken Yasny, Walter Young and the kids from Canyon School, *and for their love, patience, and support*, Miles Goodman and Sarah Gardner.

And, to my father, Stanley Gewirtz, who gave me the opportunity to embrace "one day at a time." Strangely, I am forever grateful.

INTRODUCTION

When I was growing up, I knew there was something different about my family. And it wasn't a good difference. It scared me and it made me sad. My family was full of secrets, silence, fear, and anger. I never knew exactly what was wrong, but because of the way my parents behaved, I was always afraid to bring friends home.

It is painful to grow up in a family where a parent drinks too much. So much time is spent taking care of other people and their needs that sometimes you don't know what you need. As an adult, when I came to understand that alcoholism was the problem in my family, I found out there are places a child can go for help.

If any of the situations in this book are familiar to you, beginning on page 60 is a listing of other books, people, and places that can help you.

In the United States there are 7 million school-age children who come from alcoholic families. This means that in any school classroom there are probably four to six children from this kind of family. If you are one of them, now you know you are not alone.

Carrie

The thing about my family is, they're all real crazy. If someone ever asked me to describe them, I'd make something up. I'd be too embarrassed to tell the truth. I'd lie for sure.

The truth is, in my family you can't depend on anyone for anything. Even my older brother, Warren. And he's almost seventeen. He rides a motorcycle and hides beer cans under his bed. He works in a gas station and sometimes doesn't come home until way after dinner. He smokes and pretends he doesn't. I know, because I've seen him. Once I asked him to pick me up at the Girls Club so I wouldn't have to take the bus home. He promised he would. Of course I should have known Warren would never show up. He's just like my parents in that way. I had to walk all the way home.

It was dark by the time I got to my house. My parents were already home from work. They were so mad. The minute I put the key in the door, I could hear Mamma start to swear. Dad jerked open the door and pulled me in by my arm and almost ripped it off. Both of them were yelling because I hadn't done my chores and dinner wasn't ready. Naturally, Warren wasn't around.

[9

I tried to explain, but my parents never listen to me. I should be used to it by now, but it still makes me mad. Before I started going to the Girls Club, I would have tried all night to explain why I was late. I would have cried. I would have felt real guilty, as though everything was all my fault. But now I know that my family is just nuts and totally undependable. It's not my fault.

Like the time last year when my school had Parents Day. All the parents are supposed to come to the school. Then the kids and teachers show them around. There's a play in the auditorium, and cake and refreshments in the cafeteria. Everyone gets all dressed up. The teachers put our work all over the walls.

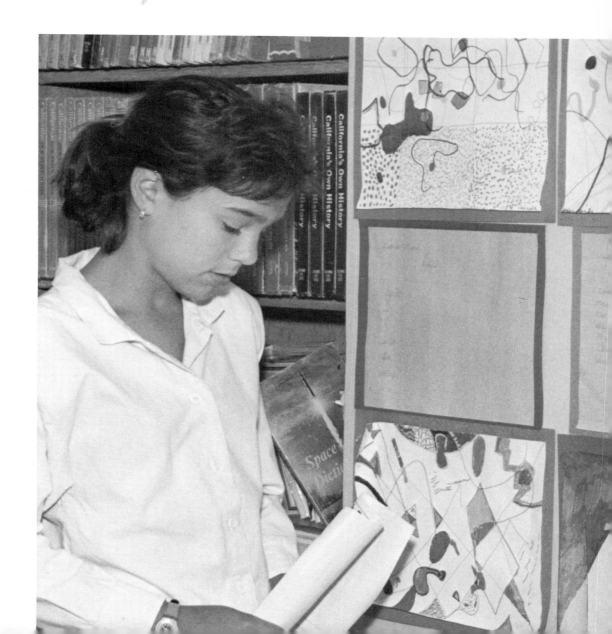

I told my parents about it. I even gave them the bulletin that was sent home. They said they would be there, but of course they didn't show up. When I asked them later why they hadn't come, they said they were so busy working they just couldn't. This year I'm going to invite Milly. She's my big sister at the Girls Club. I won't be disappointed because I know Milly always does what she promises.

Before I met Milly, I did everything my parents told me to do—even dangerous things. Like at night, when it was real late, Mamma used to wake me up. She wanted me to drive with her to the store to buy more wine and cigarettes. I used to do it because I was scared she'd get in a crash because of the way she drives when she's been drinking—all over the road. Sometimes she even goes through red lights. The car swerves and she swears at other drivers.

[13

One day at Girls Club, I told Milly about those night rides. I told her the night rides scared me but I felt like something bad would happen to Mamma if I didn't go with her. Milly made me see that there was no reason for me to be on those rides. Since I couldn't drive or anything, how could I stop an accident?

So the next time Mamma woke me up, I got up my courage and told her I wasn't going to drive with her when she was drunk because it wasn't safe. I was real scared she was going to hit me. She yelled and screamed and it woke the whole family up.

By that time I was crying. But we all agreed, even my brother, Warren, that it wasn't safe to drive with Mamma when she had been drinking. When things calmed down a little, we all agreed that she shouldn't drive at *all* when she was drunk. Dad took the keys away from her.

That night, I slept better. Maybe because I'd made up my mind never again to drive with Mamma when she was drunk. Milly said I was real brave. Maybe so, but now I wonder whether Mamma will still love me.

Joseph

Sometimes, when I get up in the morning, I find my mom asleep on the couch with the TV still on and lots of beer cans on the floor. The ashtray is always filled with tons of cigarette butts and the room smells like dead rats.

I wish I understood why she has to drink. She says her job makes her nervous and she can't sleep. She says the beer helps. It makes her sleep. Before Dad left, he used to say my mom drank so much because of him, he made her sad. But now Dad's gone and she drinks even more.

Before Dad left, he told me, "You're the oldest. It's your responsibility to see that everything runs smoothly here. Look after the little ones and take care of your mother." So I try my best.

In the morning I get up first, wash all the dirty dishes in the sink, throw out the garbage, and make breakfast. Then I wake my mom. I like to wake her before I wake my sisters and brother in case she's in a bad mood. It's better if she yells at me or hits me rather than pick on one of the little kids.

Usually, when she's mean, I try to just stay out of her way. Other times, she makes me so mad I want to hit her. She acts so different all the time. Sometimes she's real lovey dovey and goes around kissing and hugging all of us. Other times none of us can do anything right. She'll yell about the dumbest thing. Mostly, I just wish she was more like other moms and did things for us like other moms do. If I have children when I'm a grown-up, I'm sure not going to treat them like she treats us.

[16

My dad says we can live with him when he finds a house big enough for all of us. Meanwhile, there's too much work around the house for just me and I'm sick of it. It's not fair. In my friend's house everyone shares the work. So, I made a list of all the jobs that have to be done every day—things like dishes and cooking and laundry and making beds. I divided the jobs up so each of us do our share. I even gave my mom some jobs. The list won't

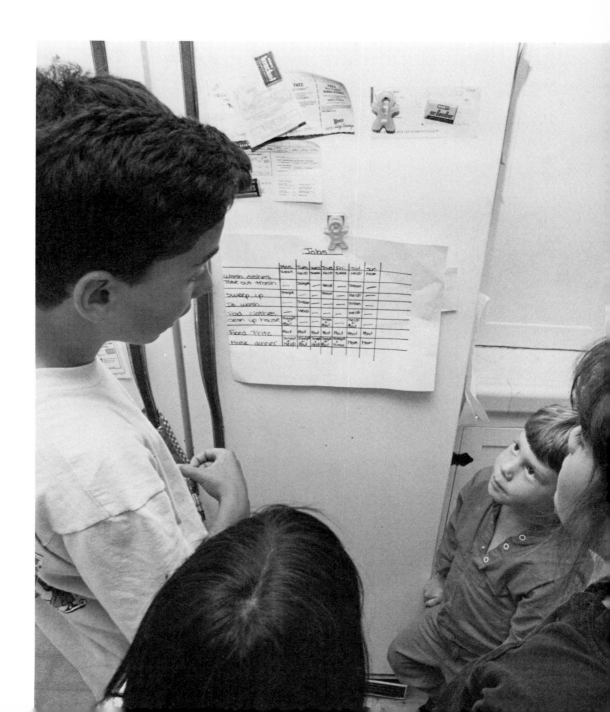

change my mom's drinking and it won't make her be like other moms. But at least I won't be doing all the dirty work. Now I'll have more time to do things I like to do, like cooking. That's something!

[18

Angela

My mommy died when I was five years old. Now I'm nine. I hardly remember her at all. My brother, Will, does though. He's twelve. He remembers her short curly hair and her big soft hands. He remembers that she smelled like butter and smiled a lot. He says she had a nice voice.

My brother remembers a lot of things. Like the time our house caught on fire. He says my daddy fell asleep with a cigar in his mouth. It fell out and the chair started to burn, then the house. I was asleep. First, a fireman dragged my brother out of his bed. Then another fireman came to get me. Will says it all happened because my daddy was drunk.

When I was six, I remember my daddy got real mad at Will for something, and chased him all around the house, Will was screaming. Then I heard a crash. Later, I found out Daddy had broken a window. He threw a chair at Will and missed. That's all I remember about that time.

Soon after that, I was living with Delores and Manny. They were my first foster parents. Until my daddy could take care of us better we had to live with foster parents. Delores and Manny had three other kids so there wasn't room for Will, too. He had to go live with other foster parents. I missed Will. I cried a lot. I missed my daddy.

Sometimes, on Saturdays, Daddy and Will would come and pick me up. We'd go out for hamburgers and french fries and stuff. We didn't talk much. Then they'd bring me back. When I kissed my daddy goodbye, I felt how rough his whiskers were. I'd stand on the front porch and watch them leave. I cried a lot. I was always scared I'd never see Daddy or Will again.

When I was seven, I went to live with the Jenkins. I liked it much better there because Will lived there with me, too. The Jenkins had two dogs and a cat. There was a big back yard with no fence. There was a pond down the road with ducks in it. I had my own room.

One day, Will ran away. Everyone was looking for him. I looked for him in the woods behind the pond. I found him. He told me he was going to keep running away until the Jenkins let him go home. I wasn't sure where my home was anymore. Will said he missed our mommy and daddy. He wanted to take care of Daddy. He cried. It was the first time I ever saw Will cry.

After that, for a while, we both went back to live with Daddy. The problem was, Daddy didn't have a job. When the light bulb burned out in the bathroom, we didn't get another one. Daddy said we didn't have enough money. We ate cereal without milk. Once I saw a mouse in the living room. I told Daddy but he just pushed me away. He was rough. He slept in his chair that night. Will said he was drunk again. When he woke up I told him about the mouse again. He threw a book at me and hit me in the head. He said the mouse was my fault because I left the front door open all the time. My head was bleeding.

The next thing I remember was going back to the Jenkins'
house. But this time Will didn't come. He stayed with Daddy. I
was scared for Will. But Will said he wasn't scared. He said he
could take care of himself *and* Daddy. Well, someone had to.

I miss Will. I miss my daddy, too. Sometimes I feel bad that I
have to live with the Jenkins instead of with my own family. But
then I remember how my dad smelled when he was drunk and I
remember the mouse in the living room. I remember how sick I
was of cereal. I remember how scared I always was when Daddy
was screaming at me.

For now, I'm used to the Jenkins. I have my own room, and
every day on my way to school I stop by the pond and feed the
ducks my leftover toast. It's not so bad. Someday we'll all live
together again. I just know it. Maybe when I'm ten.

Luther

It's hard to admit, but for awhile things were pretty disgusting at my house.

It started when Ben (he's my step-dad) left a bit of beer in the bottom of the can. When I cleaned up, I'd take a sip. The same with Mom's wine. I just sneaked a bit here and there. I kind of developed a real taste for the stuff.

At first it made me feel good. You know, after a few sips I could laugh about my crummy family. It wouldn't matter so much that Ben and Mom yelled and screamed at each other and never did anything around the house. It didn't matter that the grass in our front yard was so long the neighbors complained. The booze made me not care about anything. I didn't think so much about being alone all the time.

But pretty soon, I made friends with other kids who drank. Some of them were older and drank more than me. Some of them smoked. The more I hung around with them the more I drank. The more I drank the less I wanted to do anything else. I started to miss a lot of school. I got kicked off the basketball team for skipping practices.

I wasn't feeling so good in the mornings. Sometimes I didn't wake up until after Mom and Ben left for work. My head thumped a lot of the time and my stomach was always queasy. It was hard to eat. I always felt like I was hiding from someone and I never knew who my real friends were. That's when things were real bad.

The weird thing was neither Mom nor Ben noticed there was anything wrong with me.

One day, someone from school called up to talk to Mom. I answered. I felt pretty shaky that day. The school wanted to know what was wrong with me and why I hadn't been there for so long. I said I had a bad case of the flu. That's kind of what I felt like all the time anyway, so it wasn't really lying. The school secretary told me to have one of my parents call. Of course I didn't tell them.

Later on, the Principal called Mom at work. He told Mom I hadn't been in school for weeks and said it would be a good idea for both of my parents and me to come in for a conference with the school counselor.

None of us wanted to go. And for the longest time, we didn't. But finally, the Principal threatened to suspend me so we had no choice but to go. The counselor at school asked us all kinds of personal questions. Some of the questions we answered and some we didn't. I tried not to talk too much. I didn't trust my words.

The counselor said she thought we needed to talk to someone who could help us work our problems out *together*, as a family. She gave us the name of a clinic go to to.

My parents were so mad. They didn't think they had any problems. They thought the problems were all mine.

Well, I've started going back to school. I've seen the school counselor twice since I've been back. That's part of the deal. It's not the best time but it's not the worst, either. I didn't make any resolutions or anything, but I haven't had a drink for six days. I'm not sure about Mom or Ben, but I've decided to go to the clinic. At least once.

Jessica

We live in a big house on a wide street with a lot of trees. My father is the president of a bank. My mother is a housewife. I have one sister.

All my friends think I'm really lucky, but they don't know the truth. And if I can help it, they never will. Not even Becky, my best friend. I never bring my friends home.

In my house nothing much makes sense. Everything looks good, but really it isn't. I hate the place. We never know what to expect. Some days, my father comes home in a really good mood. Then we all smile and tell each other about our days. Some days he comes home and just slams things around and shouts.

My mother's scared of my father. She always does what he says right away. If he says, "Get me a drink," she does it. And she always has a good dinner ready when he gets home. We eat in the dining room with candles and cloth napkins. Lots of times, when he's in a bad mood, he'll look at his plate of food and start screaming and yelling. And then he throws it on the floor. Just like that! It makes me sick. Then he'll blame somebody for his bad mood, mostly me. Lots of times I get sent to my room without dinner. Then my mother starts to cry. That's a big help. All she ever does is try to convince us he's probably had a bad day or something. That makes me even madder. Why doesn't she do something?

One night at dinner, my father got so mad at me, he chased me into my room and threw me on my bed and shook me until I was crying so hard I couldn't breathe. Then he gave me this shocked look and said, "I'm sorry, I'm sorry, Jessie." And then he got on the bed and he hugged me and *he* started to cry. After that he started to touch me in places I didn't want him to—private places. Of course when I told my mother, she didn't believe me. She told me I had better not tell anyone, even my sister, because everyone would think I was nuts.

But when it happened again, I was really scared. I knew it was wrong. I had to tell someone. So I told my soccer coach. She's this really nice lady. She didn't think I was making it up or that I was nuts. She told me I was right to tell someone and that nobody should do those kinds of things to me without my permission, not even a parent.

I told my coach I was scared my father would find out I told someone and hurt me. My coach said that even though my father acts like he doesn't, he loves me. Otherwise he wouldn't hug me and cry. The thing is, he's out of control and he needs help just like I do.

My coach thought we all needed help. She has a friend who is a special kind of doctor called a *therapist*. I talked to the therapist on the phone. She helped convince me to ask my parents to set up a family meeting with her. A meeting where we could all go and talk.

It took a long time to do it. But I was so scared my father might try to touch me again, that I finally told him and my mother that I had talked to someone.

Both my parents were shocked. I asked them if they'd come to a family meeting. At first, my father yelled. My mother cried. But after awhile they agreed to go with me.

I feel a lot better knowing there's someone who we all can talk to. Maybe it will help. Everyone says it will. I hope so.

Adrienne

There's some kind of weird mix-up going on in my house and I don't understand it at all and neither do my brothers or sisters.

What happened was, last night at dinner, Papa told us he's an alcoholic. Isn't that weird? I mean, we all just about started to laugh, like he was telling us a joke or something. I mean, come on, he's nothing like an alcoholic.

I've seen those guys, they live on the street. Some of them even push shopping carts filled with all kinds of junk. Papa's just not like them.

[40

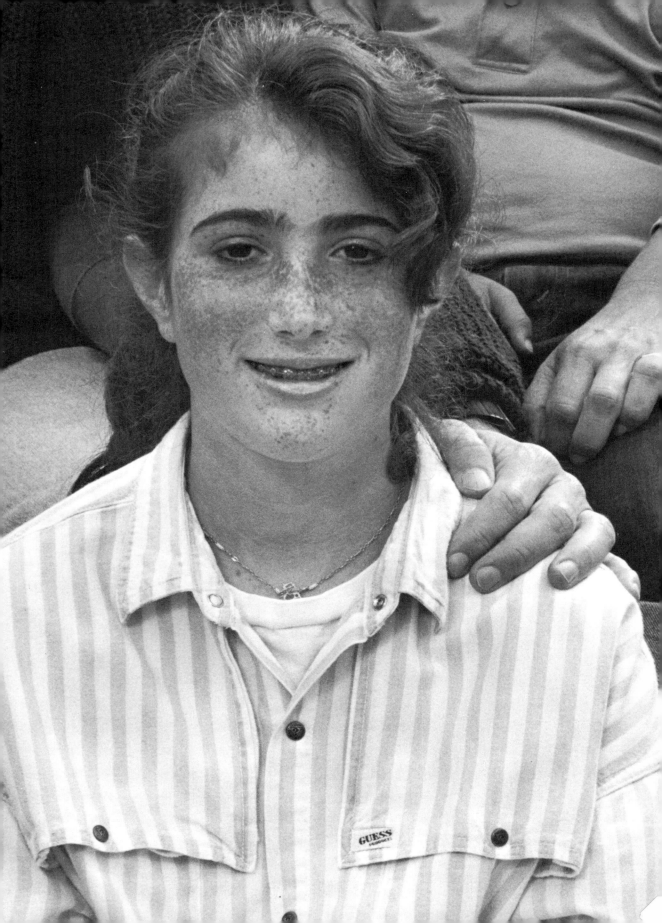

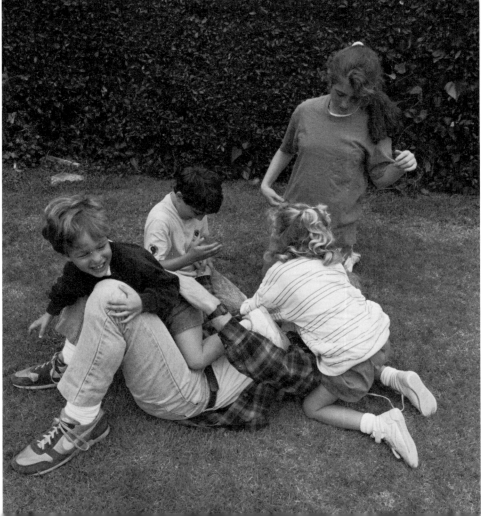

Papa is tall and handsome and always shaves and combs his hair real neat. He wears jeans and long sleeve shirts that Ma irons for him and these glasses that on other people would be nerdy, but on Papa they look smart. He needs them for reading, which he does a lot of. It's part of his job. Most of the time he stays down in his office, which happens to be in the basement of our house.

If Papa was an alcoholic wouldn't he act crazy and yell and scream and hit Ma and us kids? The meanest I've ever seen Papa was once he yelled at our dog 'cause he was lying in the middle of the doorway and Papa tripped over him and dropped a bunch of papers he was carrying.

Sometimes, before dinner in the kitchen, one of us kids will catch our folks kissing while they're cooking dinner. You know, cutting up vegetables and stuff and they just stop and kiss. I mean, who would love an alcoholic? They're usually divorced or not married at all or always mean to their wives and kids and stuff. There's just no way *my* Papa is an alcoholic.

Well, it is true that Papa doesn't always pay attention to us and sometimes stays downstairs for days. And there are times when Ma tells us we have to be real quiet, 'cause Papa's sleeping. And when I take the garbage out I see a lot of wine bottles and beer cans.

A few times, Papa promised to go places with us and then he forgot or fell asleep or something. But so what? That doesn't prove anything.

My sister said Papa slammed the basement door in her face once. My brother told me when he was small he saw Papa cry once and he says he's even seen him drunk before.

I don't know what to think.

[43

Every day now, Papa's going to these dumb AA meetings. AA stands for *Alcoholics Anonymous*. He wants us kids to go to *Alateen*. I said I wouldn't but my brother says we should. I can't understand why my brother wants to go to a meeting and sit around with a bunch of kids whose parents are drunks. My brother says I shouldn't say "drunk." He says I'm being dumb. Well, maybe I am but I never thought in a million years my own Papa could be an alcoholic.

The only reason I would ever go to one of those meetings is because maybe those kids can tell me what's going on. Maybe they understand how this could happen in my family. I sure don't.

Robert

I get in millions of fights. The kind that start with a lot of yelling and screaming. Pretty soon, someone hits someone else and there's a bloody nose or a smashed toe or something even worse.

Usually it's not me who starts the fight. Someone else will say something I don't like and I have to fight back.

Like one day at recess, right in the middle of a kickball game, Stuart asked me what kind of job my dad had. I said he was a dentist. Then Stuart said, "Well, how come if he's a dentist he's always hanging around the house in his bathrobe and slippers? And how come he never shaves or anything? I bet he's really a housewife."

So, I pushed Stuart and told him to shut up about my dad. He pushed me back. I punched him in the nose and it bled all over his white tee shirt. I liked the way the blood looked, so red. But my teacher, Mrs. Vernon, didn't. She made me stay after school and clean the blackboards. Mrs. Vernon said she was worried about me. She asked me why I'd given Stuart the bloody nose. I just shrugged.

Most of the time, I don't talk about anything that goes on in my family to anyone, hardly even my sister or brother. There's no way anyone would understand. Except for the kids in Alateen, they're different. Alateen is the group I belong to where all the kids come from families like mine. Families where someone is an alcoholic. I feel okay about telling stuff to the kids in Alateen, because everyone knows how stupid my family is and everyone else's family there is pretty stupid, too. If I didn't have them, I probably wouldn't talk to anyone.

I was glad that I hit Stuart on a Tuesday, since I go to my Alateen meeting on Tuesday nights. I could talk about it if I wanted to. The thing about Alateen is, I can talk about *all* my feelings. Not just the ones that seem easy to talk about, but the hard ones, too. It's the only place in the whole world where I'm not afraid to admit there's something wrong in my house. I know no one will hate me there. Everyone will understand. Because there's something wrong in their house, too. And we all know it stinks!

Casey

I wanted so much to be leader at the Alateen meeting the other night. I had big problems and I wanted to talk about them. But I got there late and someone else had already volunteered.

When I walked in, the volunteer was reading the *preamble*. We read it every week. The preamble tells how Alateen is for children like us. It tells how we're all getting together to help each other by talking about our problems and what we can do to make things better. It tells us we're not going to change our parents so we had better learn to take care of ourselves. We can still love them but we don't have to get stuck in their mess. The preamble is like a weekly reminder.

After the preamble, we pass around the book so each of us can read one of the "Twelve Steps" out loud. These steps are supposed to guide us. They are goals, not rules.

Finally, we choose a topic. The one we picked that night was anger. Immediately, everyone started yelling out things like "All right!" "Good topic!" "I can relate to that!" It was sure a perfect topic for me.

Nobody *has* to talk at a meeting but usually everyone wants to say something. I sure did that night. Alateen's not religious or anything like that and what we talk about is private and no one else's business. Since we trust each other, we can share our darkest secrets. That's how we help each other.

It seemed like everyone had something to say that night. Every time someone spoke about their family, it reminded me of mine and I could feel my heart start to beat real fast and I clenched by fists. After waiting and waiting it was finally my turn.

"Well, the thing of it is," I said, "I'm so mad, I can hardly talk."

Almost everybody in the group already knew that a year ago my mom left my dad because of his drinking. Me, my mom, and my little sister couldn't handle it anymore. We moved to another city. It was really hard to start all over in a new town, in a new school, and to make new friends.

Since my mom worked full time, every day after school I had to pick up my little sister from day-care. We'd come home together and I'd clean up the morning dishes and tidy up the house. Sometimes I'd make dinner and sometimes I'd order takeout food that my mom would pick up on her way home from work.

It took months and months for me and my mom to make a new life for ourselves and my little sister. It took me a long time to find out about Alateen.

"Now my dad wants us all to try it again. He wants us to move back in with him. He says he's been going to AA meetings and stuff. The thing is, I don't believe anything he says or does and I don't want to move again. I don't have any friends back there. Everyone thought I was weird because I didn't talk a lot and I spent so much time alone. Sometimes I'd just feel like closing my eyes and disappearing. I hated it. I like my life right here. I like my life without him."

Everyone in the group was quiet. The girl next to me put her hand on top of mine. The guy behind me put his hand on my shoulder. I felt like I was going to cry.

"Before you moved here, you didn't know anything about us," someone finally said.

I nodded.

"You didn't know that there was such a thing as Alateen or kids who had the same kinds of families as yours. You thought you were the only one in the world with problems like yours."

I nodded again.

"When you go back there, you're going back a different person; a stronger person. You know where to find people who will understand you and your problems."

They were right. But that didn't mean I wouldn't miss them, and I knew they'd miss me, too.

A lot of other stuff happened in that meeting and a lot of other people talked about the kinds of things that made them angry. I knew I had more hard times ahead. I couldn't lie to myself about that.

But when we closed the meeting that night, we all felt better. Even if it was only a little bit.

[59

FURTHER READING FOR CHILDREN OF ALCOHOLICS

Alateen - Hope for Children of Alcoholics. New York: Al-Anon Family Group Headquarters, Inc., 1973.
AA-based solution for children who live with alcoholism.

Black, Claudia. *My Dad Loves Me, My Dad Has a Disease.* ACT, 3010 Towncenter Drive, Suite 0-211, Laguna Niguel, CA 92677.
A workbook for younger children of alcoholics, with simple illustrations.

Brooks, Cathleen. *The Secret Everyone Knows.* Operation Cork, 4425 Cass Street, San Diego, CA, 1981.
Easy reading for the child looking for "self-help" when alcohol is a problem in the home.

Figueroa, Ronny. *Pablito's Secret/El Secreto de Pablito.* Hollywood, FL: Health Communications, Inc., 1984.

Fox, Paula. *The Moonlight Man.* New York: Bradbury Press, 1986.
Fifteen-year-old Catherine and her father take their first vacation in Nova Scotia and finally get to know each other. Catherine's father is an alcoholic.

Hastings, Jill M., and Typpo, Marian H. *An Elephant in the Living Room.* Minneapolis: CompCare Publications, 1984.
A workbook geared to grades 3-8.

Hornick-Beer, Edith Lynn. *A Teenager's Guide to Living With an Alcoholic Parent.* Center City, MN: Hazelden Educational Materials, 1984.
A highly readable book on what every teenager should know, along with practical suggestions on what to do and how to do it.

Ryerson, Eric. *When Your Parent Drinks Too Much: A Book For Teenagers*. New York: Facts on File, 1985.

This book gives good, direct advice on how to handle crises and live without guilt in the alcoholic family.

Seixas, Judith S. *Alcohol: What It Is, What It Does*. New York: Greenwillow Books, 1977.

Basic facts about alcohol in a read-alone format for seven to ten year olds along with clear illustrations.

Seixas, Judith S. *Living With a Parent Who Drinks Too Much*. New York: Greenwillow Books, 1979.

A book written to help children of alcoholics understand what is happening to them and to their families. Easy reading.

What's "Drunk" Mama? New York: Al-Anon Family Group Headquarters, Inc., 1977.

A very readable and loving story about a young girl's understanding of her father's alcoholism.

PLACES TO GO FOR HELP

Alcoholics Anonymous—World Services, 468 Park Avenue South, New York, NY 10017   (212) 686-1100.
   AA is listed in most telephone directories.

Al-Anon World Service Office, P.O. Box 862, Midtown Station, New York, NY 10018   (212) 302-7240.
   A twelve-step program that helps the husband, wife, child, or friend of the alcoholic to understand and deal with the problem. A listing for all Alateen groups in the United States is available upon written request. If there is no Alateen group in your area, Al-Anon World Services will guide you to the nearest Al-Anon group.

Children of Alcoholics Foundation, Inc., 200 Park Avenue, Thirty-first floor, New York, NY 10166   (212) 949-1404.
   This organization informs and educates the general public about children of alcoholics. It has developed an awareness program for school-age children. "The Images Within: A Child's View of Parental Alcoholism," is a display of artwork—drawings, stories, letters, and poems—by children of alcoholics which toured the United States in 1986-87.

NACOA (National Association for Children of Alcoholics),
31706 Coast Highway, Suite 201, South Laguna, CA 92677.
   This is a clearinghouse of informational and educational materials for children of alcoholics. A free information packet is available upon written request. The association name does not appear on the outside of the package.

NCALI (National Clearinghouse for Alcohol Information),
P.O. Box 2345, Rockville, MD 20852   (301) 468-2600

Kids Are Special, 525 Race Street, San Jose, CA 95126
(408) 995-6633

This organization provides community groups for children, ages four to eighteen, who are either from alcoholic or chemically dependent families. Kids Are Special services are dedicated to breaking the code of silence that exists in these families by offering a safe, nurturing place for children to go for help.

In every city there are special groups and organizations set up to help children of alcoholics. Check your local telephone book under ALCOHOLISM. There will be listings that can direct you. In some cities there may be a HOT LINE where you can get help from a special operator. Remember, you are not alone.

[63

ABOUT THE AUTHOR

Katherine Leiner grew up in an alcoholic home. She now lives in Los Angeles, California, with her husband and two children.

Ms. Leiner has written several books for children, including Ask Me What My Mother Does, Both My Parents Work, and Between Old Friends. She is currently working on a novel for young adults.

ABOUT THE PHOTOGRAPHER

Chuck Gardner specializes in human-interest photography. He lives in Westlake Village, California, with his wife and two daughters.